tate publishing
CHILDREN'S DIVISION

Dallas Becomes A Mom

Dallas

LABRADORS FOR LIFE

TERRE REDMON

Labradors for Life: Dallas Becomes A Mom
Copyright © 2016 by Terre Redmon. All rights reserved.

This title is also available as a Tate Out Loud product. Visit www.tatepublishing.com for more information.

No part of this publication may be reproduced, stored in a retrieval system or transmitted in any way by any means, electronic, mechanical, photocopy, recording or otherwise without the prior permission of the author except as provided by USA copyright law.

The opinions expressed by the author are not necessarily those of Tate Publishing, LLC.

This novel is a work of fiction. Names, descriptions, entities, and incidents included in the story are products of the author's imagination. Any resemblance to actual persons, events, and entities is entirely coincidental.

Published by Tate Publishing & Enterprises, LLC
127 E. Trade Center Terrace | Mustang, Oklahoma 73064 USA
1.888.361.9473 | www.tatepublishing.com

Tate Publishing is committed to excellence in the publishing industry. The company reflects the philosophy established by the founders, based on Psalm 68:11,
"The Lord gave the word and great was the company of those who published it."

Book design copyright © 2016 by Tate Publishing, LLC. All rights reserved.
Cover and interior design by Eileen Cueno

Published in the United States of America

ISBN: 978-1-68352-389-5
1. Juvenile Nonfiction / Animals / Dogs
2. Juvenile Nonfiction / Animals / Pets
16.07.18

This Book Belongs To:

What has four legs, a tail, is very friendly, loves to lick people, chase balls, sleep with you, and jump into the water?

Do you have any guesses?

It's a Labrador retriever.

Labradors come in three different colors: yellow, black, and chocolate. In the last few years, breeders have begun producing a fox red and silver Labrador. I have only had black and yellow Labradors, but someday I hope to have a baby chocolate born at my house.

Labrador retrievers are America's number one breed registered with the **American Kennel Club** and considered to be a favorite dog for families. They are loving, energetic, playful, intelligent, and have great athletic ability.

This story is about Redmon's Dallas Cowgirl. Dallas is a yellow Labrador retriever and came to live with us in July of 2013. She looks very white in color but is labeled a yellow Labrador by the **American Kennel Club.**

Dallas was only seven weeks old when we brought her home. She had lots of energy but slept often. Dallas learned to swim at eight weeks old, and she loved the water.

Soon, she was six months old and began getting taller, weighing more, and moving faster. She still was very white in color.

On May 31, 2014, she had her first birthday. Dallas was almost full-grown in size, but her bones and organs were not yet fully developed.

During her second year of life, she became very fond of her family. She traveled in the car, slept on their bed, and loved to play **fetch**. We took long walks, and she swam in the creeks and lakes.

When Dallas turned two in May of 2015, we knew her bones and organs were developed and she was now considered an adult dog. That summer she began jumping from the docks at the lake and could jump between fourteen to sixteen feet out over the water. Most Labradors love the water, and Dallas was no exception.

If anyone had anything to throw in the water, she would go **fetch** it. Playing **fetch** is Dallas's favorite activity. We make her sit, and then we either throw a ball or a fake retriever toy sprayed with the smell of a duck or pheasant. She has to return the item to us. She could play this game for hours.

In September of 2015, our family was ready for Dallas to have puppies. She still loved to swim and take walks, but we had to go slower. Her belly began to grow very large. One day we drove to the veterinarian and they took pictures of her belly with an **ultrasound machine**. Doctor Sarah discovered she was going to have six puppies and maybe more.

Dallas started sleeping more and eating more food. She was now feeding at least six puppies. Dallas's **mammary glands** or teats (milk glands) also grew with her. The milk glands were beginning to make milk to feed the puppies.

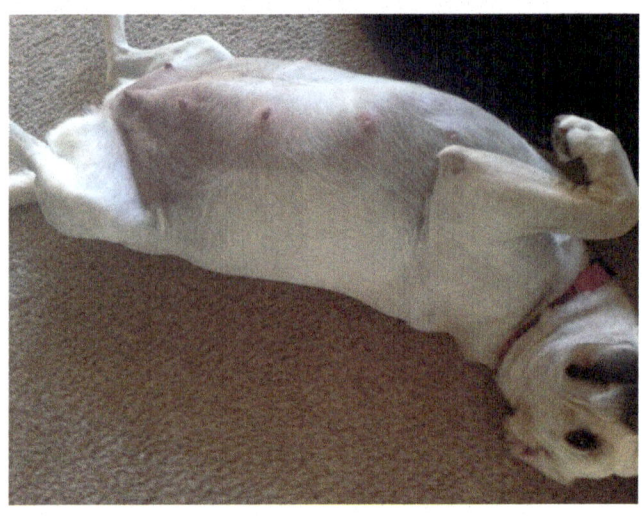

The day arrived for Dallas to have her puppies. She was very nervous. We spent most of the day outside while she dug under our deck, scratched out all the cedar shavings from her doghouse, and panted a lot. She was not in the mood to eat or play. She was trying to make a nest for her puppies.

That night she was still very nervous and finally went into our shower in our bathroom and began to relax some.

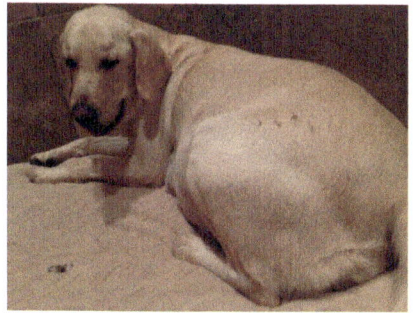

Often she would get up and pace the floor. We returned outside many more times. But finally, at 5:40 a.m., Friday, November 13, 2015, Dallas had her first puppy.

When the puppy was born, it had a tiny sac or membrane over its head. Dallas chewed on the sac, and the puppy started to breathe on its own. The puppy was very wet and slimy, and Dallas used her tongue to lick it clean and dry.

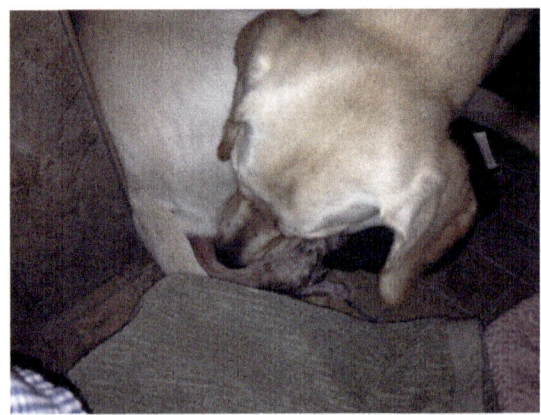

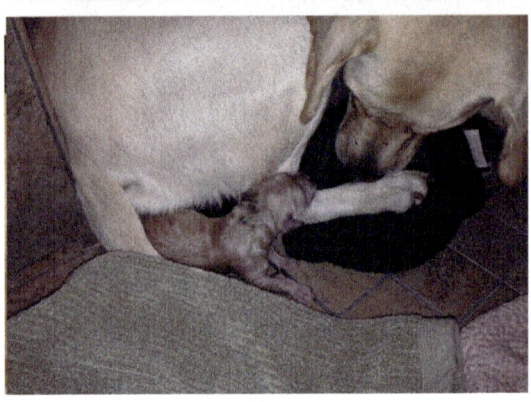

The puppy was just the size of my hand.

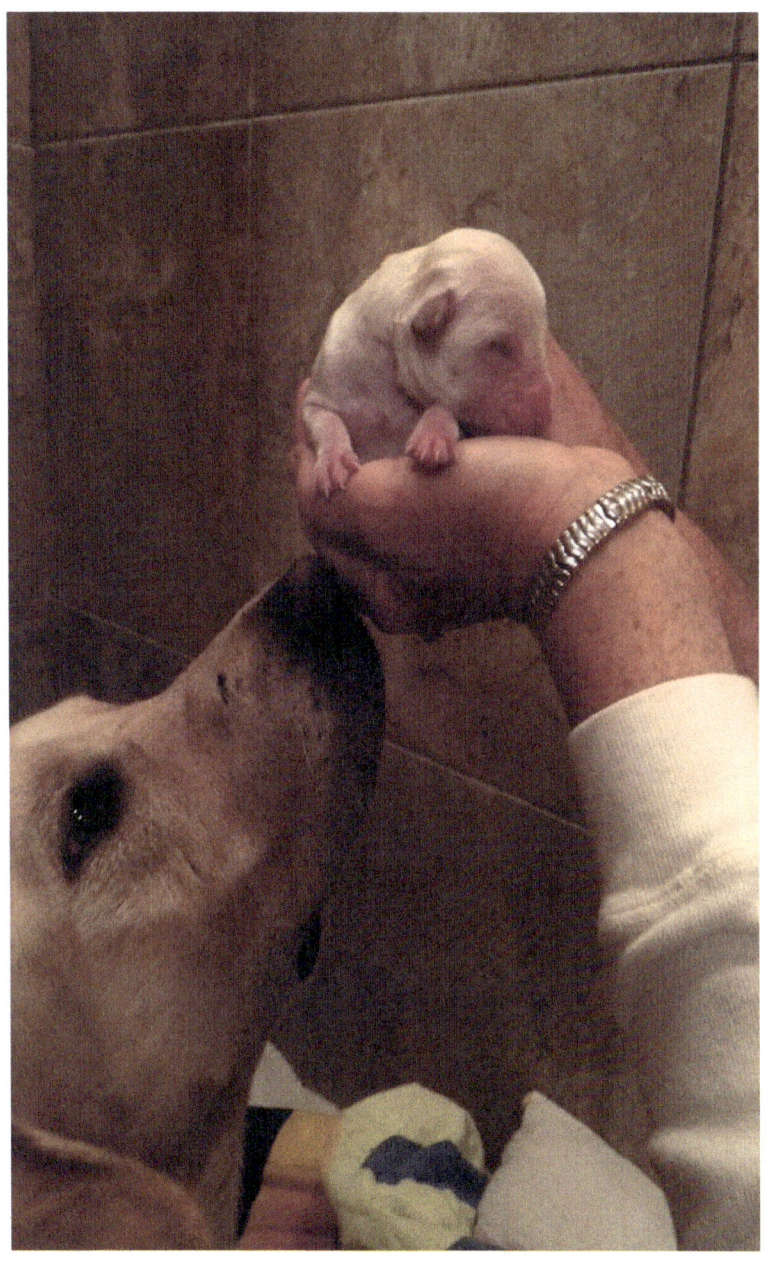

The puppies kept on coming, and soon we had seven. There were three males and four females.

At 10:00 a.m., the last puppy was born. We had four males and four females. That's eight puppies! Dallas was very tired and now began to eat her food.

The little Labradors all **nursed** from Dallas as soon as they were born and continued to **nurse** well for several weeks. They all were very healthy and ate very well.

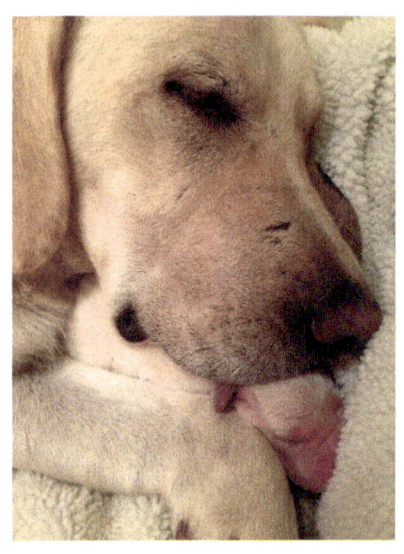

At birth, the puppies' eyes were closed and they couldn't hear. But their little noses helped them find their momma when they were hungry. They had very pink skin and looked a lot like little baby pigs.

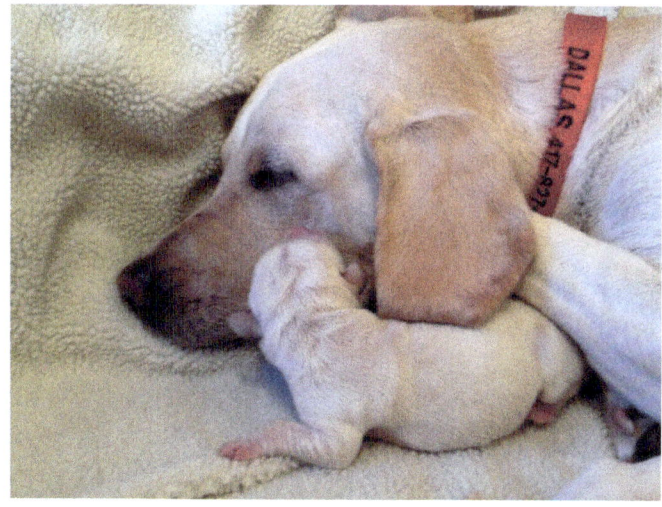

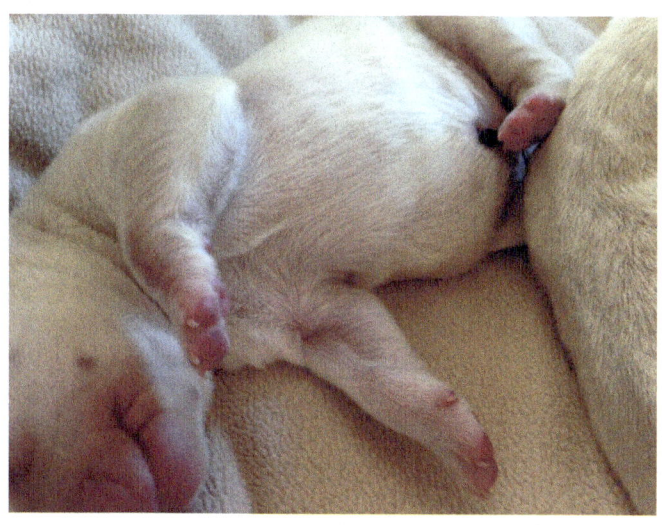

Each puppy also had an **umbilical cord**. This is their belly button, which is similar to humans. The **umbilical cord** fell off after a few days.

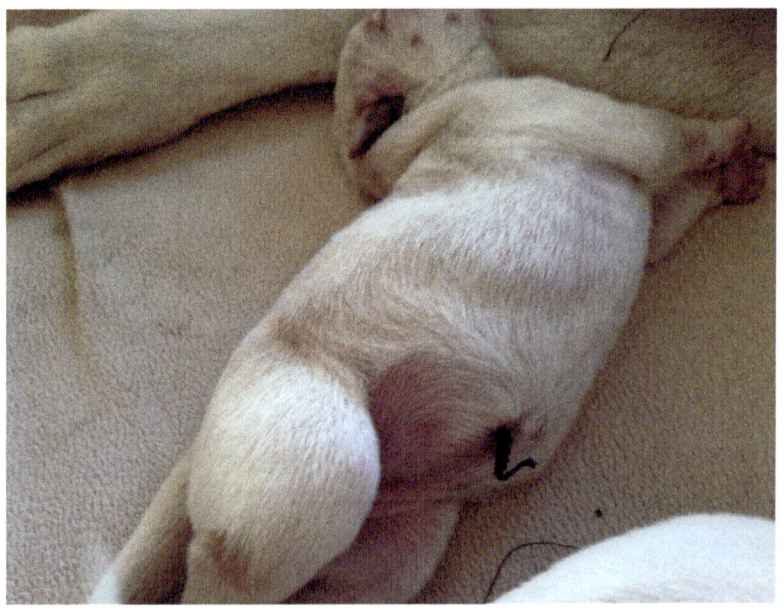

The umbilical cord looks like a piece of dark yarn

When the puppies were two days old, my daughter Stacey came to visit. Dallas greeted her and led her to the pups. After Stacey washed her hands, she held each puppy and we weighed them. The smallest pup weighed fourteen ounces and the largest weighed one pound four ounces. After that day, the babies were held each day until they left their momma.

The puppy has very tiny ears and cannot hear. The little baby is being stroked very gently.

Dallas was a proud momma. She loved her new bed and enjoyed spending time with her puppies. She washed them often and taught them how to pee and poop by licking them. She then would clean the cage by eating their poop and licking the urine or pee up. She kept the babies very clean.

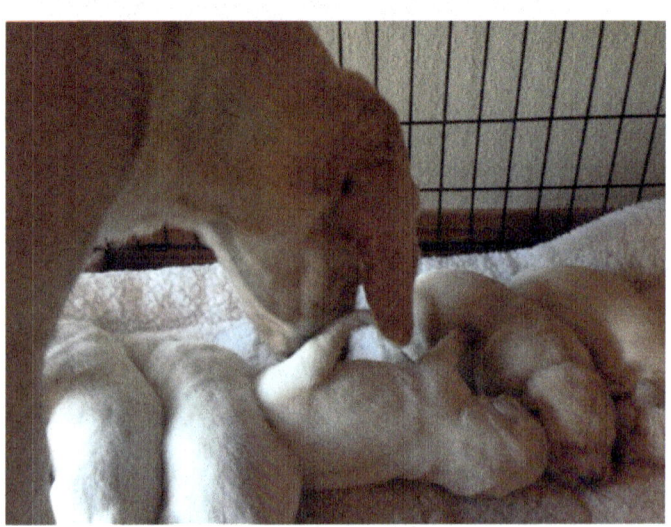

When the puppies were three days old, they had their first checkup at the vet. At this time, they all fit in a small plastic tub. The veterinarian removed their extra toenail by freezing it off. This is called **dewclawing**. The toenail is removed so dogs don't get the toenail caught on fences, logs, and other outside objects.

Doctors Laura and Denise said, "These are the healthiest puppies we have ever seen for this young age. They are so big!" They both thought Dallas was being a great mom and taking extremely good care of her babies.

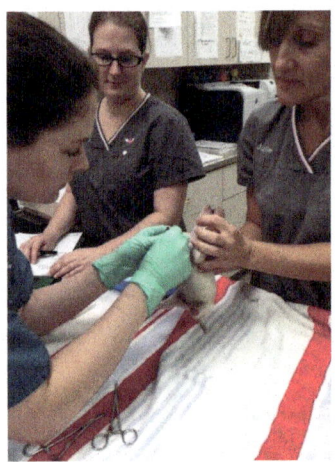

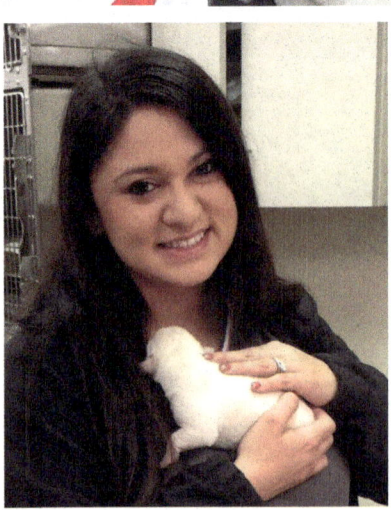

Veterinarian assistant calming the puppy after its toenail is removed

The puppies continued to grow for the next few weeks. Their eyes began to open around fifteen days old, and they also began to hear sounds. By the time they were three weeks old, their pink noses and feet were beginning to turn black and teeth were developing in their mouth.

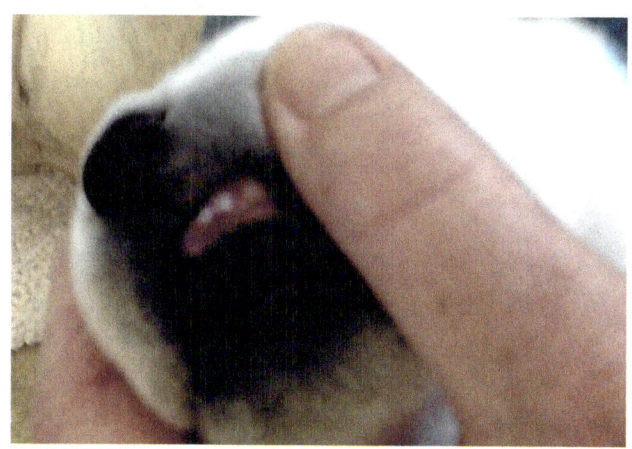

We had to clean a lot for the puppies and Dallas to keep the area healthy for them. Two times a day we cleaned and washed the bedding from the cage and mopped the floor every night. We did this type of cleaning until the puppies were four weeks old.

Once again the puppies had lots of visitors and loved all the extra human attention. From three to fourteen weeks, **socialization** is very important. Positive contacts, like petting, holding, speaking softly, and playing with the puppy will help the puppy become a better companion for others later in life. However, it is extremely important to limit contact to individuals and animals outside the home since puppies have not had their **vaccinations (puppy boosters)**.

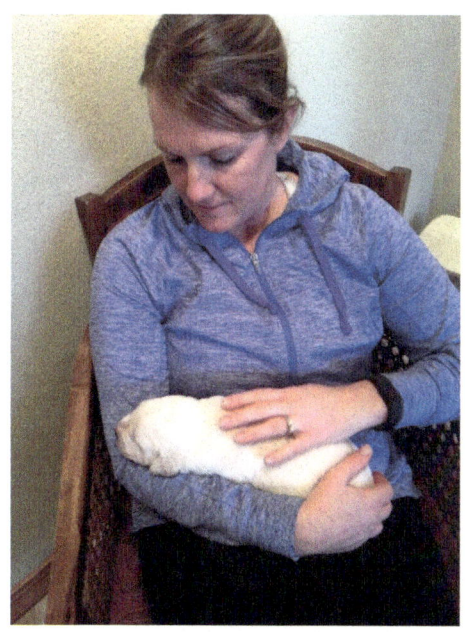

Lots of affection will help the puppies adjust to their new owners, after they leave their litter mates.

At this time, each puppy was wearing a colored collar, except for one who we had named Hoss. He had a little white spot on his head, so we could tell him apart from his litter mates. Most of the time they slept and **nursed** from Dallas. The pups continued to eat very well, and I started introducing them to solid food. They ate wet puppy food at first, and then I began to mix the dry food in with the wet.

When they were four weeks old, the smallest weighed six pounds one ounce and the largest, whose name was Hoss, weighed seven pounds and seven ounces.

We moved the puppies downstairs, where they could get to go outside. They were a little scared at first but soon learned there were many things to explore and see in the great outdoors.

They played hard and became experts at eating from a bowl. Sometimes they even fell asleep in the bowl after a big chase with each other.

The horses Danny Boy and Blue were very curious about the puppies. They would come to the fence to watch the little fur balls play in the grass.

One day, the eight puppies got a ride in the red wagon, which took them to their doghouse.

Pulling the wagon with the little pups was a little difficult. They kept jumping out, and I kept putting them back in. Finally we arrived at their doghouse.

The doghouse had cedar shavings and was very warm for them. I covered the outside of the house with a large tarp so the wind would not blow through the cracks of the house. They slept in the doghouse during the daytime, and at night, we brought them back to their special room in the house.

At night, my son Kevin would visit and bring them upstairs to play with, pet, and feed. I always had to give the kitchen floor an extra wipe down on those nights.

The little yellow Labradors were now five weeks old. The smallest was a little girl named Pink Collar, who was later named Shelby. She weighed nine pounds and twelve ounces. The largest was now twelve pounds and seven ounces. Hoss weighed eleven pounds and nine ounces. The biggest puppy was named Bad to the Bone and was later named Tye by his owner.

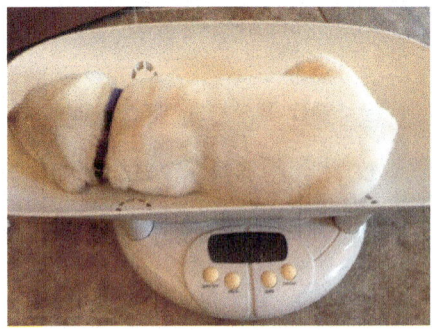

Bailey being weighed at five weeks. She weighed eleven pounds and twelve ounces

Hoss enjoying his chew toy

Cleaning for the puppies was a little more difficult. Newspapers had to be laid down with extra bedding. The puppies learned to pee and poop on the newspapers, but it was quite a mess in the morning. Cleanup up was a chore each day, and boy, did it smell in their indoor pen. The puppies continued to grow and grow, and we kept them outside as much as possible!

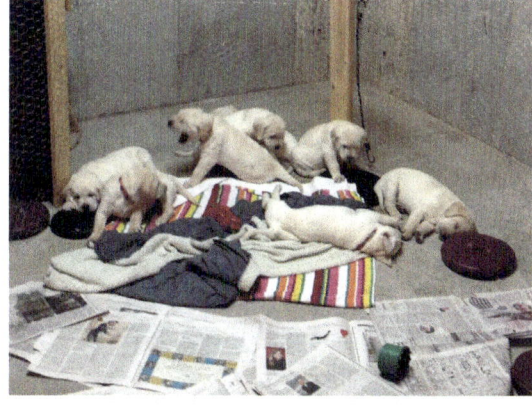

The puppies were about ready to go home with their owners. Each puppy had been sold when they were three weeks old. We made another trip to the veterinarian at six weeks. We put our large dog crate at the back of the Suburban and then put the puppies in two at a time. We had to work fast because they wanted out so bad. Soon we were on our way and the puppies began to relax, and they quickly fell asleep.

When we arrived at the vet, my daughter and I carried the crate into the office. We were sent to a large room, and Dr. Denise began checking the puppies one by one. Once again she was surprised how healthy and big the puppies were. She listened to their hearts, checked their teeth and ears, and weighed each one.

At this time they were given their first **vaccinations (puppy boosters)** and given some worm medicine. When puppies are little, they often get worms or parasites from their mother when they are nursing. If the worms are not treated, puppies will become **infested** with the worms and become extremely sick and may die. When the puppies are nine weeks old, their owners will take them back to the veterinarian for more **vaccinations (puppy boosters).**

At seven weeks, the puppies' new owners began arriving and taking their new puppy home with them. Hoss was the first one, then Remington, Daisy, Tye, Lucy, Shelby, Bailey, and then Tuff.

Lucy and her new owners

Bailey's new family

Bailey got to fly on an airplane to the state of Connecticut and loved all the attention she got. She got to hang out at the airport and received lots of friendly pats from people walking by. She even got to go to a restaurant!

Bailey on board the plane.

It was a little sad when all the puppies left, but Hoss comes to visit every day. He lives with my daughter Stacey and her son Parks. Every morning I go to their house and get him while she is at work. Puppies need lots of attention after they leave their litter mates so they don't get lonely. **Socialization** is still important at this age.

Terre giving lots of snuggles to the puppies before they leave

Hoss enjoying time with his family.

Raising a litter of puppies is a big commitment. But in the end, it is very rewarding to watch these little fluff balls grow and change on a daily basis. I think I might make it my new hobby.

I'm sure there will be more litters of puppies at our house in the next few years. A new puppy recently has arrived at our house. We named her Cali and she is a black Labrador. Hopefully when she is full-grown she will be able to have puppies like Dallas.

Cali's first day at her new home.

Do you think Dallas will like her?

I think she does!

Based on my experience, Labradors do make a great family dog. We have had eleven different Labradors during the past thirty-five years. Their names are Buck, Skipper, Pepper, Foxy, Tar, Molly, Buddy, Jazz, Duke, Elle, and Dallas. We had seven black Labradors and four yellow Labradors. Each one of these dogs were and still are very special to us. I can't imagine not waking up to a wet Labrador kiss each morning.

Glossary

American Kennel Club. A registry of purebred dogs and pedigrees in the United States. A pedigree is a lot like a family tree. It describes where the dog is from.

dewclawing. The removal of the extra claw on the inside of a dog's paw. The dewclaw is up higher than rest of the claws and can get caught on objects.

fetch. To go after and return something.

infested. To spread in a bad way. When animals are infested there is a good chance they will become ill. Animals can become infested with ticks, fleas, or worms, which are called parasites.

mammary glands. Is an organ inside a female mammal that produces milk to feed her young. Dogs can have up to ten mammary glands or teats.

nurse. To take milk from the teat of the mother dog.

socialization. Enjoying being around others and developing pleasant social relations.

ultrasound machine. A machine used by doctors to view the inside of dogs or humans to see everything from organs to puppies. Can take pictures also.

umbilical cord. Provides nourishment to an unborn mammal before it is born. The mother breaks the cord with her teeth right after the puppy is born.

vaccinations (puppy boosters). Helps the body fight against diseases or illness. Vaccinations help your pet live a long healthy life.

Source: *Webster's Dictionary*

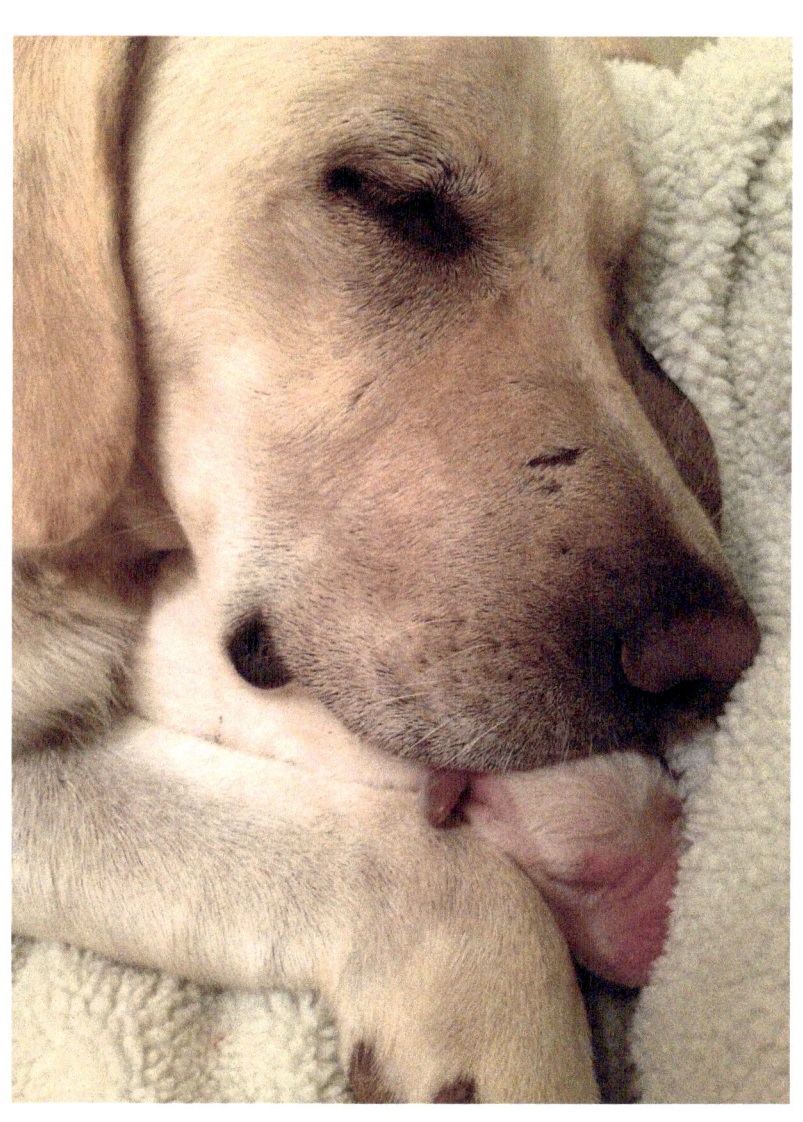

Hoss

THE END

Cali

listen|imagine|view|experience

AUDIO BOOK DOWNLOAD INCLUDED WITH THIS BOOK!

In your hands you hold a complete digital entertainment package. In addition to the paper version, you receive a free download of the audio version of this book. Simply use the code listed below when visiting our website. Once downloaded to your computer, you can listen to the book through your computer's speakers, burn it to an audio CD or save the file to your portable music device (such as Apple's popular iPod) and listen on the go!

How to get your free audio book digital download:

1. Visit www.tatepublishing.com and click on the e|LIVE logo on the home page.
2. Enter the following coupon code:
   5801-20b4-3fdd-69f7-8c8d-01fa-0a68-53b8
3. Download the audio book from your e|LIVE digital locker and begin enjoying your new digital entertainment package today!

CPSIA information can be obtained
at www.ICGtesting.com
Printed in the USA
LVOW01s2025120816
499726LV00006B/6/P